Cracking the German Code

by Rena Korb

PEARSON

Scott
Foresman

Editorial Offices: Glenview, Illinois • Parsippany, New Jersey • New York, New York
Sales Offices: Needham, Massachusetts • Duluth, Georgia • Glenview, Illinois
Coppell, Texas • Ontario, California • Mesa, Arizona

Opener: ©DK Images; 1 Corbis; 3 Library of Congress; 4 Library of Congress; 6 ©DK Images; 8 ©DK Images; 10 ©DK Images; 13 ©DK Images; 14 ©Hulton Archive/Getty Images; 17 Library of Congress; 18 National Portrait Gallery, London; 19 ©DK Images; 21 Corbis; 23 Imperial War Museum/©DK Images

ISBN: 0-328-13467-8

4 5 6 7 8 9 10 V0G1 14 13 12 11 10 09 08 07 06

World War II

In the 1930s a new power had appeared and was rising in Europe. Under the leadership of Adolf Hitler and the Nazi party, Germany had been growing stronger and stronger. The Nazis grew to be so powerful that Germany started to claim land that did not belong to it. German troops took over Austria and part of Czechoslovakia. The leaders of Europe allowed Germany to keep the new areas. They wanted to avoid war. Germany, however, took over the rest of Czechoslovakia.

On September 1, 1939, the German army invaded Poland. Bomber planes streamed through the sky and tanks rolled across the borders. Two days later—even before Poland surrendered— Great Britain and France declared war on Germany. World War II had begun.

Adolf Hitler, leader of Nazi Germany

More than twenty countries fought in World War II. On one side were the Allied powers made up of Great Britain, Russia, the United States, and their supporters. On the other side were the Axis powers, which included Germany, Italy, Japan, and their supporters. Only a few countries in the world did not take sides. By the time World War II ended in 1945, fighting had happened in parts of Europe, the Pacific, Asia, and North Africa.

After the German armies captured Poland, they began their attack on the rest of Europe. Within months, Germany had taken over much of the continent. By the summer of 1940, only Great Britain stood against Germany. The other Allied powers joined Great Britain later.

The Germans bombed Britain. They threatened them with invasion. They sent bomber planes to fly over the cities and

countryside. German submarines, known as U-boats, sank ships taking supplies and soldiers to Britain. Germany sent thousands of war plans and messages each day by radio. All of these messages were in Germany's secret code. British officials knew they could fight the Germans better if they could decode, or read, these secret messages. Then Britain could find out Germany's next plan of attack. The British had known about this code for years, but they never thought they would be able to break it.

Officers from the Allied powers of the United States and Britain shake hands.

Secret Codes in History

Since the invention of writing, people have put their messages in codes to keep them safe from opponents. For instance, some **ancient** Greeks used cylinders to help them read secret messages. The sender would write a message on a strip of paper that was wrapped around a cylinder. The receiver of the paper strip would wrap it around a cylinder of the exact same size to read the secret message.

Other message systems would replace one letter with another. This was called a cipher, or code, system. A key showed how the letters were substituted so the message could be read. In the late 1400s Leon Battista Alberti from Italy thought of using a disk to put messages into code. This made cracking coded messages difficult. Each letter of text was represented by several different letters in one message. In the early 1900s, inventors started to use machines to help them create complicated codes.

This is an example of an early cipher text.

The Enigma

Shortly after World War I, a German inventor developed a code machine for business purposes. In the 1920s the German military used a version of that machine, now called an Enigma, to code military messages. *Enigma* means "mystery." The machine was made so that only someone with an identical machine could decode the message.

This Enigma machine is ready to use.

The Enigma looked a bit like a typewriter. The Enigma operator typed a message on a regular keyboard. When the operator pressed the key for the letter A, for example, electrical signals were sent along a system of wires. These wires connected to three wheels. At each wheel, the letter A changed to a different letter.

Wires also connected the keyboard and the wheels to sockets that scrambled the letter even more. Then an electrical current went to a lampboard with small windows that lit up. Each window had a letter. When the electric current reached the lampboard, the coded letter lit up. The operator would see that A had become another letter, such as D.

After one key was pressed, the wheels turned in a pattern. When the operator pressed the key for A again, a new letter, something other than D, appeared on the lampboard. The code looked like random letters. Having more than one code for each letter disguised the message even more.

The Enigma was a very complicated machine. Each of the three wheels could be interchanged, or switched, and each wheel had a ring of letters that could be put in a different order. Also, the wires on the lampboard swapped letters even more. With the wheels and the lampboard, the Enigma had more than 150 million different settings! Today it would take a computer an entire year to test just one message on all the possible settings. No wonder the Germans thought that their codes would not be cracked!

A . −
B − . . .
C − . − .
D − . .
E .
F . . − .
G − − .
H . . . .
I . .
J . − − −
K − . −
L . − . .
M − −
N − .
O − − −
P . − − .
Q − − . −
R . − .
S . . .
T −
U . . −
V . . . −
W . − −
X − . . −
Y − . − −
Z − − . .
1 . − − −

To send secret messages, an Enigma operator typed in each letter of the message with one hand. With his other hand, he wrote down the letter that lit up on the lampboard. He then gave the coded message to a radio operator, who sent it to a receiver by Morse code. Morse code is a way of communicating letters and numbers through long and short signals. These letters are printed out as dots and dashes. The receiver typed in the coded message on his Enigma, and the original letters appeared on the lampboard.

The German military gave Enigma operators codebooks telling them how to set up their machines. Each day they had to put their wheels in order, set the wheels so that the correct letter appeared through the window, and plug in the wires. Codebooks gave the operators directions so that all Enigma machines were set exactly alike.

2 · · − − −
3 · · · − −
4 · · · · −
5 · · · · ·
6 − · · · ·
7 − − · · ·
8 − − − · ·
9 − − − − ·
0 − − − − −

These dots and dashes stand for letters and numbers in Morse code.

Polish Code Breakers

Even before World War II, a small group of scholars in Poland was trying to learn the secrets of the Enigma code. They didn't know how the machine worked. They couldn't crack the code.

Their luck changed in 1931. Hans-Thilo Schmidt, who worked in the German government, sold documents describing the Enigma machine to the French government. The French gave this information to Polish officials. With this information, a Polish mathematician named Marian Rejewski figured out how to build a working model of the Enigma. The first piece of the puzzle had been solved!

Polish code breakers spent a year studying the machine. Finally they could crack the daily code. This let them decipher, or figure out, the messages that the Germans were sending.

Soon Enigma machines and codes became more complicated. It was difficult for the Polish people to figure out the messages. Shortly before World War II began, Polish officials decided to tell the British government how Enigma machines worked. At a secret meeting, the Polish people gave the British two Enigma machines they had built.

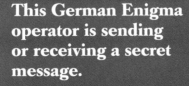

This German Enigma operator is sending or receiving a secret message.

Bletchley Park

Britain's government had thought that Enigma codes could not be broken. The information from Poland changed this way of thinking. The British quickly set up a new code-breaking center at an old mansion called Bletchley Park. The British hired thousands of people to work on cracking the Enigma's code.

Many workers were professional cryptologists, or people who study and break codes. Others had worked as clerks. Some worked for the military. Some were **scholars** in mathematics, science, or languages. There were both men and women. These people all had one thing in common: They were experts at solving problems and puzzles.

Cryptologists puzzled day and night over the German messages. The old mansion was almost like a **temple** to them. The work they did was top secret. The British did not want the Germans to know they might break the Enigma's code. The cryptologists could not tell their friends or family about the important job they did. There were even people at Bletchley Park who did not realize they were working on cracking the German code!

Bletchley Park

Breaking the German Code

The British code breakers did not have German codebooks. So they had to figure out how the Enigma was set each day. Enigma operators changed their wheels at least once per day. They sent that day's starting point as a three-letter code to the receiver two times in a row.

The code breakers used these repeated letters to find **links.** A link would help them make better guesses about the settings of the wheels. Then they tested these settings by hand until they found the right one. The code breakers went through this process each day.

Once the daily code was cracked, the work of deciphering the messages began. One group of people in Bletchley Park **translated** the messages from German into English. Another group of people checked the messages for German war plans. They sent the news to the British government and to military leaders.

The system used at Bletchley Park let the British know about secret German war plans. The Bletchley system, however, was a lot of work because the German military changed its codes all the time. Sometimes the Germans even made changes to the Enigma machine itself.

British Prime Minister Winston Churchill paid a surprise visit to the code breakers at Bletchley Park in September 1941.

The Genius of Alan Turing

A man named Alan Turing was already working hard to find new ways to break the code. As a scholar at Cambridge University, Turing had been a **seeker** of mathematical knowledge. Now Turing tried to find a new way to **uncover** the secret German code.

Turing studied messages that had already been deciphered. He saw that many messages included the same words in the same places. Turing called these repeated words and phrases "cribs." One example of a crib was *wetter*, the German word for "weather." The Germans sent a weather report every morning. It almost always contained the word *wetter* at the beginning. Turing started to collect these messages.

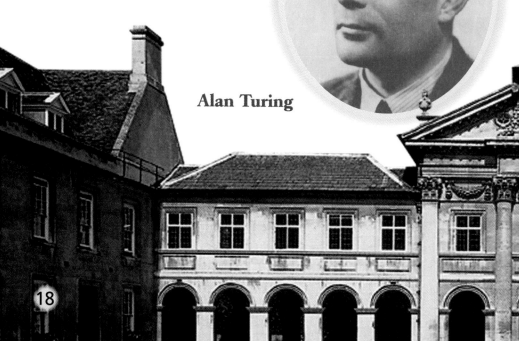

Alan Turing

The next step was to examine the messages for a place where the word *wetter* could fit. The Enigma could not code a letter as itself. That meant the letter *W* in the original text could never match up to the letter *W* in the coded text. Finding the location of the crib was a big step in breaking the code. Code breakers had a clue to find the settings of the Enigma each day.

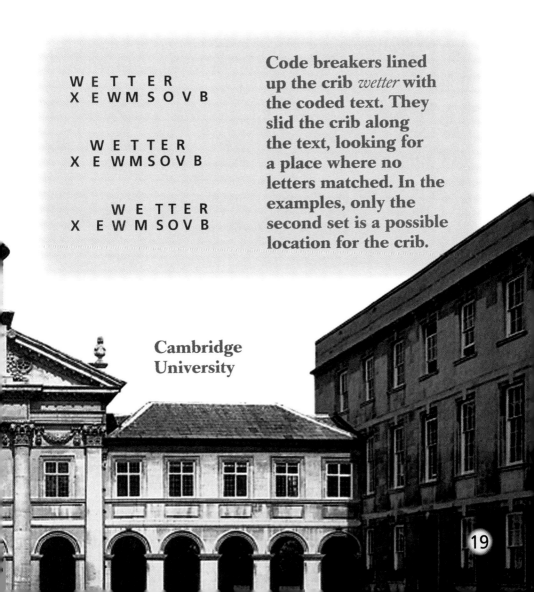

W E T T E R
X E WM S O V B

W E T T E R
X E WM S O V B

W E TT E R
X E W M S O V B

Code breakers lined up the crib *wetter* with the coded text. They slid the crib along the text, looking for a place where no letters matched. In the examples, only the second set is a possible location for the crib.

Cambridge University

19

This crib worked, but it took a lot of time. Turing invented a machine to do part of the job. Called the Bombe, this machine looked for the places where cribs could fit in the message. Sometimes the Bombe could find the correct place within an hour. Other times it took days.

The Bombe was more than six feet high and seven feet long. It weighed two thousand pounds. By the end of the war, Britain was using more than two hundred of these amazing machines.

In February of 1942 the German navy added a fourth wheel to the Enigma. This made their codes more complicated. It took Bletchley Park code breakers nearly nine months to crack the code. Until the new codes were broken, the Allies could not track German U-boats. The U-boats sank many ships.

Two naval victories greatly helped the code breakers in World War II. In October of 1942 British destroyers forced the crew of a German U-boat, the U-559, to abandon ship. Three British sailors boarded the ship and retrieved codebooks. This helped figure out messages. A couple years later in June of 1944, American ships forced the crew of a German submarine, the U-505, to abandon ship as well. The Americans captured the submarine and its codebooks. The captured codebooks were sent to Bletchley Park.

In 1944 Americans captured a German U-boat, the U-505.

The Fall of the Axis Powers

By 1942 the United States had joined the Allies in World War II. With the help of the United States, the Allies fought to free land that Germany and the other Axis powers had captured. In June of 1944, the Allies landed forces in western Europe while the Russian armies pushed the German army out of Russia. By fall, German forces retreated. The Allies invaded Germany, and its leaders surrendered. World War II finally ended in 1945.

Being able to decode secret German messages helped the Allies in their long, difficult fight. The code breakers gave information that helped military leaders make decisions about when and where to attack the Axis powers.

RELY ON THE QUALITY...
ballito
STOCKINGS

The D

No. 14,078

Broadcasting: Pag

TO-DAY

Germany Signs

PREMIER TO BROA
AT 3 p.m.: THE KING

Synchronising Keeps You

TO-DAY is V-E Day. The war in Europe is over. Germa terms of unconditional surrender to Britain, the Uni Russia at 2-41 a.m. D.B.S.T. yesterday at Gen. Eisenhow Rheims. The German war has lasted five years, eight mo.

The Ministry of Information announced last night:—

It is understood that in accordance with arrangements between the three Great announcement will be broadcast by the Prime Minister at three o'clock to-r May 8 [that is, to-day].

In view of this fact to-morrow, Tuesday, will be treated as Victory in Europe (V-E regarded as a holiday. The day following, Wednesday, May 9

His Majesty the King will broadcast to the to-morrow, Tuesday

The Code Breakers in History

Once the war ended, you might think that the code breakers got the credit they deserved. They did not. The British government refused to let anyone know about the code breakers' hard work. The government closed Bletchley Park and burned or hid all clues about what had taken place there during the war. They even destroyed all the Bombes.

Nearly thirty years later, government leaders changed their minds. Finally, Great Britain uncovered the secret of the code breakers and their **triumph** over the German code.

The *Daily Dispatch* announces the end of World War II, or *Victory-Europe Day*.

Glossary

ancient *adj.* of times long past.

links *n.* things that join or connect.

scholars *n.* people who have much knowledge.

seeker *n.* one who tries to find; one who searches.

temple *n.* a building used for worship.

translated *v.* changed from one language into another.

triumph *n.* victory; success.

uncover *v.* to make known; reveal; expose.